DATE DUE

Demco, Inc. 38-293

The Battles of Lexington and Concord

CORNERSTONES OF FREEDOM

SECOND SERIES

Heidi Kimmel

Children's Press®
A Division of Scholastic Inc.
New York • Toronto • London • Auckland • Sydney
Mexico City • New Delhi • Hong Kong
Danbury, Connecticut

Photographs © 2007: Art Resource, NY: 3 (Bridgeman-Giraudon), 8, 44 bottom (New York Public Library); Bridgeman Art Library International Ltd., London/New York: 11 (Historical Society of Pennsylvania, Atwater Kent Museum of Philadelphia), 16 (Museum of Fine Arts, Boston, gift of Joseph W. Revere, William B. Revere, and H. R. Revere), 4, 18 (Private Collection), 6 (Edward Truman/Massachusetts Historical Society, Boston, MA, USA); Corbis Images: 25 (Burstein Collection), 20 (Hulton-Deutsch Collection); Getty Images/Stock Montage: 30; North Wind Picture Archives: cover, 7, 10, 14, 19, 22, 24, 28, 31, 35, 36, 39, 44 top right, 45 left, 45 right; Stock Montage, Inc.: 12; Superstock, Inc.: 40 (Blerancourt, Chateau/Lauros-Giraudon, Paris), 15, 26; The Art Archive/Picture Desk: 27 (Global Book Publishing), 32 (Laurie Platt Winfrey), 5, 21, 44 top left.

Illustration by XNR Productions, Inc.: 29

Library of Congress Cataloging-in-Publication Data
Kimmel, Heidi.
    The Battles of Lexington and Concord / Heidi Kimmel.
        p. cm. — (Cornerstones of freedom. Second series)
    Includes index.
    ISBN-10: 0-516-23627-X
    ISBN-13: 978-0-516-23627-8
    1. Lexington, Battle of, Lexington, Mass., 1775—Juvenile literature.
2. Concord, Battle of, Concord, Mass., 1775—Juvenile literature. I. Title.
II. Series.
    E241.L6K49 2006
    973.3'311—dc22   2005024563

CHILDREN'S PRESS, CORNERSTONES OF FREEDOM™,
and associated logos are trademarks and/or registered trademarks of
Scholastic Library Publishing. SCHOLASTIC and associated logos
are trademarks and/or registered trademarks of Scholastic Inc.

1 2 3 4 5 6 7 8 9 10 R 16 15 14 13 12 11 10 09 08 07

By the rude bridge that arched the flood,
Their flag to April's breeze unfurled,
Here once the embattled farmers stood
And fired the shot heard round the world.
—from "Concord Hymn," by Ralph Waldo Emerson

When dawn broke on the morning of April 19, 1775, a group of farmers, artisans, merchants, and professionals assembled in Lexington, Massachusetts. They had no idea what to expect. They only knew they were prepared to commit **treason** to protect their rights.

By nightfall, the **patriots** discovered that they could not only stand up to the British, they could also defeat them. The shots had been fired that proclaimed the birth of liberty, and eventually these shots would be heard and celebrated not only in the thirteen American colonies, but throughout the world.

BOSTON HOLDS A TEA PARTY

It wasn't the first time colonists had taken matters into their own hands. Problems started in 1764, when the British began imposing taxes on goods that the colonists used every day, such as sugar, coffee, paper, and newspapers. Some colonists believed these taxes were unfair because the colonies had no representation in the British government. The British retracted most of their taxes by 1770 but one remained—the tax on tea. When angry colonists started **boycotting** British tea and **smuggling** untaxed tea into the colonies, the British responded with the Tea Act of 1773. This law changed the way tea was sold in the colonies. For one thing, colonists could buy tea only from the British East India Company. Patriots feared Britain was taking more and more control of the colonies' economy. They chose to take back control.

> ## To the Public.
>
> THE long expected TEA SHIP arrived laſt night at Sandy-Hook, but the pilot would not bring up the Captain till the ſenſe of the city was known. The committee were immediately informed of her arrival, and that the Captain ſolicits for liberty to come up to provide neceſſaries for his return. The ſhip to remain at Sandy-Hook. The committee conceiving it to be the ſenſe of the city that he ſhould have ſuch liberty, ſignified it to the Gentleman who is to ſupply him with proviſions, and other neceſſaries. Advice of this was immediately diſpatched to the Captain; and whenever he comes up, care will be taken that he does not enter at the cuſtomhouſe, and that no time be loſt in diſpatching him.
>
> New-York, April 19, 1774.

This notice about keeping a tea ship from docking in New York kept the public up to date.

The patriots decided to refuse shipments of tea. It was abandoned to decay in warehouses in Charleston, South Carolina. Ships headed for New York and Philadelphia had to return to Britain without unloading their tea. But when the British ships the *Dartmouth*, *Eleanor*, and *Beaver* sailed into Boston Harbor loaded with tea on November 27,

Governor Thomas Hutchinson was determined that British ships would enter Boston's port.

1773, the Massachusetts governor ordered that the three ships stay in the harbor until the colonists paid the taxes on the tea.

Governor Thomas Hutchinson, a British loyalist (a person who supported the king), proclaimed that if the tea was not unloaded by December 17, he would have customs officials unload it and auction it off to those who were willing to pay the taxes. The Sons of Liberty—an organization of colonists dedicated to separating the colonies from England—tried to pressure the governor into changing his mind. He refused.

Samuel Adams, a leader of the Sons of Liberty, decided it was time to act. On December 16, 1773, one day before the

* * * *

governor's deadline, thousands of Boston's citizens met at the Old South Meeting House. When Adams announced the pre-arranged signal, "This meeting can do nothing more to save the country," a group dressed as Mohawk Indians entered the room and invited those in attendance to join them.

That night, between 60 and 120 men disguised as Mohawk Indians and armed with hatchets and clubs headed to Griffin's Wharf, where the *Dartmouth*, *Eleanor*, and *Beaver* were docked. There, they boarded the three British ships and dumped 342 chests loaded with tea into Boston Harbor.

The Old South Meeting House, where the Boston Tea Party was planned

This engraving by Paul Revere shows Boston Harbor, where chests of tea were dumped on the night of December 16, 1773.

In New York and Philadelphia, patriots pledged to take the same action if British cargo ships docked in their harbors.

What came to be called the Boston Tea Party lit the fuse in a struggle that would explode at Lexington and Concord.

INTOLERABLE PUNISHMENT

As word of the destruction of the tea spread to other colonies, many colonists pledged they would follow Boston's example. But when word reached England, King George III decided that Boston's colonists deserved harsh punishment for their illegal actions. Parliament, Britain's lawmaking body, passed many acts designed to do just that.

The Boston Port Act closed Boston to all shipping and trading until the British East India Company was repaid for the cost of the tea. The Administration of Justice Act stated that British officials and soldiers accused of a capital crime while performing their duties in the colonies could be sent back to England to stand trial. The patriots called this the Murder Act, because it gave British soldiers the means to escape colonial justice. The Quartering Act extended the requirement that colonists provide lodging for British troops at their homes as well as in empty houses, inns, and other public buildings. The Massachusetts Government Act made General Thomas Gage, already chief of British forces in the colonies, the governor of Massachusetts.

The British labeled these acts collectively the Restraining Acts. But the colonists dubbed them the Intolerable Acts.

ENGLAND'S PRIZE

Prior to June 1, 1774, Boston was one of England's economic prizes. Its port was a major shipping center, home to an enormous fishing industry and a large whaling industry. Shipbuilders and all the other trades supporting these industries were abundant. The city was bustling with lawyers, merchants, and tradesmen. Coffee shops and taverns did a lively business.

But on June 1, when the Boston Port Act went into effect, shop windows were shuttered and church bells rang out a funeral **dirge** from morning until night. Public buildings were draped in black bunting, and Boston's citizens, dressed in black clothing, prayed and **fasted**.

The other colonies also mourned. Virginia's governing body, the House of Burgesses, proclaimed the day was to be

9

Colonists who became increasingly unhappy with British control over their affairs often met to discuss what actions to take. Meetings like this one led to the idea for the First Continental Congress, which assembled in September 1774.

marked by fasting and prayer. In Philadelphia, the **clappers** of the church bells were muted, and dummies representing tax collectors were burned by furious mobs. Baltimore traders refused to trade with England any longer. New York dockworkers refused to unload British ships. From all over the colonies, food and supplies began to pour in to Boston. The Boston Port Act united the colonies as nothing had before.

THE FIRST CONTINENTAL CONGRESS

In September 1774, representatives from every colony except Georgia met at Carpenter's Hall in Philadelphia to attend the First Continental Congress, a meeting to discuss what colonists should do next. The delegates split into two groups: those who wanted to negotiate a peaceful resolution with the king, and those who wanted total independence from Britain. Although they knew they could be accused of treason, on October 14, they approved the Declaration and Resolves, written by Thomas Jefferson, which would later become a model for the Declaration of Independence. This

document said that Parliament had no right to pass laws for the colonies. On October 26, the First Continental Congress decided to meet again on May 10, 1775. Most of the delegates did not expect that before they met again, the first shots of the American Revolution would be fired.

MASSACHUSETTS GETS ORGANIZED

For the ten months the port of Boston was closed until the day troops marched to Concord, Boston sat idle, its warehouses empty. Most of the city's businesses had been forced to shut their doors. Angry mobs roamed the city's streets.

Colonists in Massachusetts burned papers and other taxed items to show their refusal to pay taxes to England.

Random and not-so-random attacks on loyalists and British troops were common. The citizens were losing everything they had worked for.

While the First Continental Congress was in session, colonists were busy selecting delegates to the Massachusetts Provincial Congress, which would serve as the government of all of Massachusetts outside of British-controlled Boston. Considered an illegal body, it replaced the Massachusetts House, which had been **disbanded** by the British. With John Hancock as its president, the congress wasted no time in passing three important measures. Massachusetts towns would set up militias consisting of fifty soldiers and an appropriate number of officers to lead them. Massachusetts would no longer pay taxes to England. And Committees of Safety would be established, whose purpose would be to spread information quickly among the colonies.

During the winter of 1774–75, men between the ages of sixteen and sixty-five formed militias, led by veterans of the French and Indian War (1754–63), which conducted drills regularly. The men had no uniforms and had to wear their everyday clothes. They were armed with their hunting weapons. Many towns called meetings and voted to impose taxes on themselves to pay for wagons to transport cannons and for collecting and stockpiling ammunition. Many townspeople brought guns to secret hiding places, lending or donating them to the cause.

In Boston, the colonists despised the British soldiers. Colonists insulted the soldiers, and children threw snowballs at them. Citizens and soldiers picked fights with each other on the streets and in taverns. British soldiers began deserting in large numbers after the patriots organized a secret operation that safely transported deserters out of Boston. Tension was in the air. Both sides waited for something to happen, but neither wanted to be the one to begin armed conflict.

SECRETS AND SPIES

Massachusetts patriots established a network of spies. These men met secretly at the Green Dragon Tavern in Boston. All participants swore an oath on a Bible at the beginning of each meeting not to reveal what was said. While it is not known

BEHIND THE RED COATS

British soldiers were called Redcoats because of their red uniforms. Although handsome, the uniforms were made from itchy wool, and the soldiers were forced to wear them on even the hottest days. The high collars often scraped their skin until it bled.

Dr. Joseph Warren of Boston

who all the spies were, it is known that Sam Adams and John Hancock were present at these meetings.

On the afternoon of April 17, 1775, Dr. Joseph Warren, one of Adams's most trusted colleagues, was not seeing patients, but rather spying on General Thomas Gage. Warren was the most prominent member of Boston's Committee of Safety. He had received word that on April 15, Gage had removed his best troops from their normal duties in order to give them special training. These companies were fast-moving and could be used to go out into the surrounding towns on a strike and return quickly. Rumors had been circulating throughout the colony that the British would soon march on Concord. Colonists put weapons and supplies on wagons and moved them to other towns or hid them in swamps. Colonial minutemen, militiamen who could be ready to fight at a moment's notice, were put on alert.

This famous portrait of Paul Revere shows him at work as a silversmith.

It was rumored that the king had ordered Gage to disrupt illegal meetings, seize illegal weapons, and arrest John Hancock and Sam Adams. The two men and a number of colonial leaders had just attended a meeting of the Provincial Congress, which was held in Concord, to choose representatives to the Second Continental Congress.

THE COMMITTEE OF OBSERVATION

Paul Revere was one of the most trusted members of Adams's inner circle. In addition to being a silversmith, engraver, maker of false teeth, political cartoonist, and newspaper writer, Revere had organized a network of post riders (postal employees) from towns outside of Boston who would carry warnings throughout the entire colony. He had also organized a group of thirty patriots, known as the Committee of Observation, to spy on General Gage. That very morning, several of them had observed Major Edward Mitchell, accompanied by twelve officers, ride out of Boston toward Concord.

They were headed to Concord because a few weeks earlier, General Gage had found out about the supplies and weapons that had been secretly stockpiled there. He learned of this through one of his spies, who later reported the locations and size of the patriots' supplies. Gage may have decided that the time had come to deal with the traitors. He would have his troops arrest Hancock and Adams, who were rumored to be in Lexington, 12 miles (19 kilometers) from Boston. Then the troops would continue 4 miles (6 km) on to Concord and take the supplies the British could use back to Boston. They would destroy the rest. Gage may have believed that once Hancock and Adams were arrested and tried for treason, the other colonists would come to their senses and begin acting like loyal British citizens again.

In mid-April, the British warship *Somerset* had been moved into the mouth of the Charles River, and patriot spies

PAUL REVERE'S RIDE

On April 19, 1860, poet Henry Wadsworth Longfellow wrote the poem, "Paul Revere's Ride," to capture the spirit of Revere's service.

LISTEN, my children, and you shall hear
Of the midnight ride of Paul Revere,

. . . .

He said to his friend, "If the British march
By land or sea from the town to-night,
Hang a lantern aloft in the belfry arch
Of the North Church tower as a signal light,—
One, if by land, and two, if by sea . . .

So through the night rode Paul Revere;

. . . .

To every Middlesex village and farm,—
A cry of defiance, and not of fear,
A voice in the darkness, a knock at the door,
And a word that shall echo forevermore!

PART OF THE TOWN OF BOSTON IN NEW ENGLAND AND BRITTISH SHIPS OF WAR LANDING THEIR TROOPS 1768

A view of Boston, with British warships filling the harbor

heard the crew lowering its longboats into the water. This suggested that perhaps the British would be using them to ferry their troops from Boston to Cambridge, on the opposite shore. From there, they would march north to Lexington. Or they could decide to march across the land bridge, the Boston Neck, that led out of Boston, a distance of 21 miles (34 km). Crossing the river, however, would cut 5 miles (8 km) off the trip.

The patriots would probably not know the route the British would take until the last minute. All Revere knew for sure was that by the time the route was known, British troops would seal off the city, preventing riders from leaving to spread the alarm. He could only hope his plan to avoid this possibility would work.

THE PLAN UNFOLDS

By late in the afternoon of April 18, 1775, Paul Revere had received enough reports from his spies to spur him to action. He began to carry out his plan. Revere went to see the **sexton** of the Old North Church, Robert Newman, an unemployed shoemaker. Then he visited a **vestryman** of

While this British soldier endured the taunts of colonial children, British officers were making plans for their troops to seal off Boston.

Thomas Bernard, who played an important role in the events of the night of April 18, 1775

the same church, Captain Pulling, and another patriot, Thomas Bernard. He told each of them to be prepared for an operation that evening. He also prepared two friends—boat builder Joshua Bentley and shipwright Thomas Richardson.

Meanwhile, Dr. Warren learned that the crew of the *Somerset* had seized all of the ferries and boats on both banks of the Charles River. He knew the time had come to visit his best source, no matter how dangerous. From this source, he learned that the march would be that very night, the destination was Concord, and the route was by water.

THE BRITISH PREPARE

At 9 P.M. British officers quietly entered the barracks where soldiers from the divisions Gage had been training were sleeping. They were ordered to dress quietly in the darkness. Seven hundred British regulars, or soldiers, were then assembled on the Boston Common and marched down to the banks of the Charles River. It took around two hours for all of the troops to cross. In fact, it took so long that the British commander, suspecting that the countryside might be warned, sent back word that reinforcements should be dispatched.

Meanwhile, Warren had three options. A man on horseback could ride across the Boston Neck and around to the road leading to Concord. But it was very likely that British sentries, or guards, would stop any rider. A rider could cross the Charles River by boat, then continue on horseback down the Concord Road. However, the crew of the *Somerset* might catch anyone attempting to cross. Or, someone could send a signal from Boston to Charlestown, on the other side of the Charles River, and from there, a rider could leave for Lexington and Concord. But the danger was that the signal might be seen by the British.

A British regular in full uniform

21

Two lanterns in the steeple of the Old North Church signal that the British are approaching by sea.

Warren decided to take no chances. He would employ all three methods to warn Lexington and Concord of the Redcoats' approach. He summoned Paul Revere and Billy Dawes.

Billy Dawes was a **tanner,** an excellent rider, and a dedicated patriot. He arrived at Warren's home before Revere. Warren sent Dawes out with a message for Adams and Hancock. Dawes was to take the land route. By the time Revere arrived, Dawes had started out. Revere wasted no time in setting out to meet up with Newman, Pulling, and Bernard. He told them to follow their prearranged plan and display two lanterns in the church tower, meaning the British were coming by sea.

As Bernard stood guard outside the church, Newman got out two lanterns he had hidden in a closet. He and Pulling each hung one around their necks and proceeded to climb almost fourteen stories to the highest window in the steeple. Using **flint**, they got a flame going in a tinderbox, then lit the candles and placed them in the lanterns. They opened the window and for just an instant directed their lantern lights toward Charlestown.

NIGHT RIDERS

Patriots posted on the opposite shore saw the lights, and a rider headed out for Lexington. Others rushed off to get a horse for Revere. Some rode off to warn the people of Cambridge. Meanwhile, Newman and Pulling descended in total darkness, hid the lanterns, and almost ran into British troops passing in front of the church. They then groped their way to a window near the altar, climbed out, and disappeared into the night.

Revere headed to his home to pick up things he would need for his own ride: heavy coat, boots, spurs. Danger was in the air. British soldiers were headed for Boston Common. Revere had hidden a boat under a wharf in the North End. At a little after 10 P.M., he headed out to meet up with Richardson and Bentley, who would row the boat across the Charles River.

The three managed to sneak past the *Somerset* and land on the Charlestown shore. There, the patriots waiting for Revere assured him that the signal from the lanterns had been spotted. Revere mounted the horse they had waiting for him. Brown Beauty was known to be an unusually fast,

After patriots saw the lights from the Old North Church, Paul Revere rode off to warn his fellow colonists.

★ ★ ★ ★

A view of Boston's North End, where Paul Revere hid a boat under a wharf.

strong, and tireless mare. A little after 11 P.M., Revere set off traveling quickly, but not so quickly as to attract attention to himself. The British had set up a series of roadblocks and had already arrested those traveling on the roads. Without warning, Revere saw two British soldiers dash out of the darkness and block his path. He and Dawes had earlier concluded that if they were recognized, the soldiers would not hesitate to shoot them. Revere was forced to turn his horse and flee, with one British soldier attempting to chase him down.

But Revere and Brown Beauty soon got away from the pursuer and continued on a long, roundabout route toward Lexington. At each town he passed through, Revere knocked on shutters and banged on doors, shouting, "Turn out! Turn out! The regulars are out!" Then the post rider would sleepily struggle into his clothes, saddle his horse, and gallop off to the towns he was responsible for rousing. In each town, another post rider would set out on his appointed rounds—on and on, in an ever-widening network that spread out from Charlestown to the north and west. And in each town, the militia would line up on the village green and prepare to march off to where the confrontation would take place. The townspeople rang bells, beat drums, and shot signal muskets. On through the night, through dozens of villages, the message was delivered: "The regulars are out!"

Paul Revere and Brown Beauty awaken a colonist to warn him of the approach of British troops.

Buckman's Tavern, where militiamen awaited word from Paul Revere, as it appears today in Lexington, Massachusetts

CONVERGENCE AT LEXINGTON

A little after midnight, Paul Revere rode into Lexington. He hurried to Buckman's Tavern, where many militiamen were waiting for word. He then proceeded on to the Clarke **parsonage,** where Adams and Hancock were staying with Hancock's relatives. The two knew the time had come to pack up and leave Lexington or face arrest by the British. Revere learned that the rider who had received the lantern signals in Charlestown had not arrived, and he assumed the man had been captured by the British. Revere believed the two lanterns in the Old North Church had been an unsuccessful

A militiaman prepares to leave his worried family and face the British in battle.

signal after all. Dawes had also not arrived, but Revere was relieved when he walked in thirty minutes later.

The militiamen at Buckman's Tavern had awakened all the militiamen of Lexington, and they assembled on the village green. Lexington's express riders headed out. There were so many that Revere and Dawes were forced to leave for Concord on two exhausted horses, instead of fresh ones they'd hoped to get. On the road, they met Dr. Samuel Prescott, who offered to help them spread the alarm.

Shortly after that, however, they ran into British major Edward Mitchell, who had been hanging around the Concord Road since eight o'clock the previous morning. Mitchell had

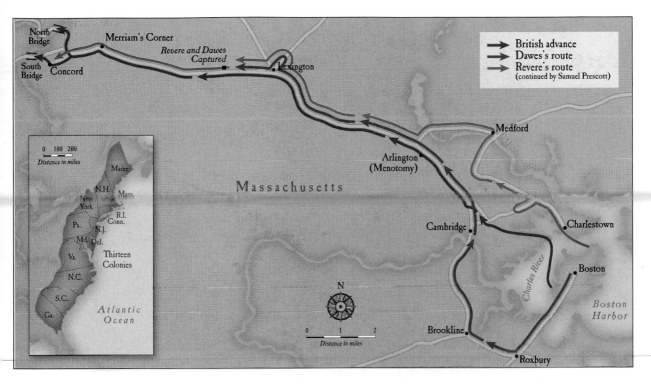

rounded up only four militiamen in his makeshift detention center in a fenced pasture. He forced Revere, Dawes, and Prescott to join them. At a prearranged signal, however, the trio made a break for it. Prescott jumped a wall on his horse and escaped. Dawes's horse bolted and threw him, but Dawes managed to escape by crawling into some brush, later returning to Lexington on foot.

Revere, who was surrounded by ten British soldiers, admitted who he was. He told Mitchell the militia throughout the entire area had been alerted and the British regulars were marching into a trap. Since Mitchell had heard the church bells ringing and the alarm shots, he believed Revere and decided to head back toward Boston and warn the British regulars. He took Brown Beauty with him and

★ ★ ★ ★

left Revere and the four others to walk back to Lexington.

THE WAR BEGINS

When Revere reached Lexington, he believed he would be able to rest. But much to his surprise, Hancock had not left yet. He had wanted to stay and fight with the militia. Hancock was finally convinced that his skills were needed more in Philadelphia, so Hancock, Adams, Revere, and John Lowell, Hancock's secretary, got into Hancock's carriage and headed off to a home near Woburn. Then Revere accompanied Lowell back to Lexington to retrieve Hancock's trunk, which had been left behind and was filled with incriminating papers that would be needed at the meeting of the Second Continental Congress.

As Revere and Lowell rode into Lexington, they observed a scout informing patriot Captain John Parker that the British troops were less than 1 mile (1.6 km) away. The captain had warning shots fired, and the militiamen returned to Lexington Common and lined up, two abreast. Parker looked out over the seventy-seven or so militiamen lined up in front of him. They were mostly ill-clothed. Some were

John Hancock

British troops fire on the colonists at Lexington in the first battle of the American Revolution.

armed with fowlers (long hunting rifles), others with shorter muskets or antique guns or swords, and some had no weapons at all.

Revere and Lowell crossed through the ranks and entered Buckman's Tavern. It was around 5 A.M. and dawn was breaking. From the window of the tavern, Revere saw the advance unit of the British troops marching quickly to the village green. At their head was Major John Pitcairn. Captain Parker gave the colonists his final instructions: "Don't fire unless fired upon. But if they want a war, let it begin here."

The British troops had probably been expecting a larger group of patriots than the approximately seventy-seven they found assembled on Lexington Common, since they had been hearing the alarms being sounded all night. Pitcairn, on horseback, shouted at the militiamen, "Throw down your

As two British regulars watch for approaching colonial militia, their fellow troops march on Concord.

arms. Ye villains, ye rebels." Seeing that they were greatly outnumbered, Parker ordered his men to put down their weapons and scatter. Although some did not throw down their arms, many militiamen had turned and were walking away when a shot rang out. The British had fired a volley without an order from their officers.

Colonel Francis Smith arrived with the remainder of the British troops as British soldiers charged the colonists with their bayonets, fired their guns, and threatened to invade private homes and Buckman's Tavern. The troops would not obey their officers and halt. Smith ordered that a drummer play "Down Arms" repeatedly. Finally, the soldiers did as they were told.

Eight militiamen lay dead on the green, and nine others were wounded. Few of the colonists got off any shots. The

British suffered almost no casualties. Major Pitcairn's horse received two wounds, and a private was slightly wounded. There were many who witnessed what happened: the militia-men, the British troops, bystanders, and women and children watching from the windows of their homes. To this day, there is still disagreement about who fired the shot that would change the history of the world. Perhaps the most well known of the witnesses was Paul Revere himself. He and Lowell were carrying the trunk out of Buckman's Tavern, bullets hissing past their ears. Revere later reported:

> *While we were getting the trunk, we saw the regulars very near, upon a full march. . . . In our way we passed through the militia. There were about fifty. When we had got about one hundred yards [91 meters] from the meeting-house, the British troops appeared. . . . In their front was an officer on horseback. They made a short halt when I saw, and heard, a gun fired, which appeared to be a pistol. Then I could distinguish two guns, and then a continual roar of musketry; when we made off with the trunk.*

ON TO CONCORD

Once order was restored, Colonel Smith had his men line up in columns. He informed his officers that they were going on to Concord to locate and demolish hidden weapons, ammunition, and supplies. Some of the regulars thought that after the violence that had just occurred and the unruly behavior of the troops, perhaps they should head back to Boston. The countryside had been stirred up, and thousands of farmers would be able to severely cripple a British force of seven hundred. But Smith was determined to carry out his orders. He allowed his men to fire a victory salute in the air and give three cheers before they marched out of Lexington, headed for Concord.

The British troops were impressive as they marched along in perfect unison, drums beating, wearing their fine uniforms. Everyone knew of their great victories in Europe and the Americas. As they watched the British approach the town, the Concord militiamen, knowing that militias from other towns were on their way to join them, decided to occupy the high ground on the other side of the North Bridge, one of two bridges leading out of Concord. This high ground was known as Punkatasset Hill.

THE SEARCH FOR WEAPONS

At 7 A.M. the British halted. Some of the troops went to guard the South Bridge. Others remained in town to search for weapons. Smith ordered some of the remaining troops to take possession of the North Bridge. They were to cross that bridge and proceed to the Barrett farm, because loyalists had informed them that weapons were hidden there. The companies at the North Bridge, commanded by Captain Walter Laurie, positioned themselves 800 yards (732 m) from where the colonists were stationed on Punkatasset Hill. The colonists looked down at them, and waited.

Major Pitcairn forced colonist Ephraim Jones at gunpoint to reveal the location of two cannons hidden in the town. After disabling the cannons, Pitcairn returned with

Smith's troops burned gun carriages to keep the patriots from using them in battle against the British.

Jones to Jones's inn and ate breakfast. Meanwhile, Colonel Smith searched for more weapons and waited for troops under the command of Lord Hugh Earl Percy to arrive. As militia companies from surrounding towns began to arrive, the colonial presence at North Bridge swelled to around five hundred men. The British regulars at the bridge, numbering around one hundred, sent an urgent message to Smith to send reinforcements.

But Smith continued searching for weapons. After finding only 500 pounds (227 kilograms) of musket balls and some wooden gun carriages, he had the musket balls thrown into a pond. (They were recovered by the patriots the next day.) Smith then had a fire built and burned the gun carriages. But the fire spread to the roof of the courthouse. Rather than

Colonists fire upon British troops at the bridge at Concord.

burn down the town, Smith had his troops help the townspeople put it out.

Unfortunately for Smith, the militiamen posted at the North Bridge under Major John Buttrick thought the British were burning Concord. The colonial commanding officers wondered how to proceed. They had no instructions from the Provisional Congress, and the Second Continental Congress had not yet met. They were just a group of farmers, craftsmen, and merchants watching their town and their rights go up in flames.

Major Buttrick asked Colonel James Barrett, who had returned from hiding weapons and other supplies stored at his farm, for permission to go back to Concord to prevent it from burning down. Captain Isaac Davis, leading a group of militiamen who had come from Acton, told Barrett, "I haven't a man that's afraid to go." Barrett ordered the militiamen to take control of the North Bridge and march into town. He instructed them not to fire unless the British fired first. Buttrick was given command of the attack. He ordered the colonists to line up in two columns and move toward the bridge.

SHOWDOWN AT NORTH BRIDGE

The British troops stationed there were outnumbered four to one. Captain Laurie was hoping that his troops' muskets could overcome the colonists' advantage. British muskets, which were more than 4 feet (1 meter) long, had a longer range than the weapons the patriots were using. Laurie decided to line up his troops on the same side of the bridge the colonists were approaching from. He quickly realized this was a mistake and began to withdraw across the bridge. On the way, several British troops tried to remove some of the bridge's planks in order to slow the patriots' advance, but it was too late.

The British fired several warning shots into the river. Then they fired a volley at the colonists. Captain Davis and a militiaman from Acton fell dead. By some accounts, the British disregarded their orders by firing on the patriots, showing lack of discipline. The five hundred colonists waited for

★ ★ ★ ★

Major Buttrick's orders. Then at the words, "Fire, fellow soldiers; for God's sake, fire!" they fired the first round. In the first volley, four of the eight British officers, plus three regulars, fell. Despite the shouted commands of their officers, the British lines, greatly outnumbered, broke and ran back to Concord. For the first time, the patriots realized their power: they could force the British troops to retreat.

REGROUPING AND RETREAT

On their retreat back into town, Captain Laurie's troops met up with Colonel Smith and reinforcements. The patriots continued crossing the bridge and took up positions on a ridge overlooking it. As the British troops who had been searching the Barrett farm returned to the bridge, the colonists allowed them to cross without firing. In the heart of Concord, the British took care of the wounded and got their troops in order to march. Almost two hours passed, but Smith delayed, waiting for reinforcements to arrive. Finally, he couldn't delay any longer. Militiamen were arriving from all over the area. By the end of the afternoon, there would be divisions from as far away as New Hampshire.

As the British troops left Concord around noon, Smith could look up at the surrounding hills and see them covered with patriots, now more than 1,500 strong. Smith's troops had no extra rounds of ammunition. Smith sent **flankers** out on both sides of the road to keep the militiamen out of shooting range.

But about 1 mile (1.6 km) out of Concord, the flankers arrived at a crossroads known as Merriam's Corner, where a

★ ★ ★ ★

stream crossed the road. The British troops had to cross a bridge there, which allowed the militiamen to get close to them. The militiamen began firing on the British troops. From there, and for the 22 miles (35 km) back to Boston, the British faced the challenge of fresh militiamen arriving and taking up positions along the road, firing at them from behind every rock, tree, and wall.

As the British continued their retreat, they came upon Colonel John Parker and the Lexington militia, some of them wearing bandages from their earlier encounter. The Lexington militiamen attacked with such ferocity that the British were brought to a momentary halt. Among those wounded was Colonel Smith himself. Flankers eventually pushed the Lexington militiamen back.

As they continued on their way, the British troops dropped their muskets, ammunition, heavy coats, bayonets,

George Washington, general of the colonial army, would later become the first president of the United States.

drums, fifes, cartridge boxes, and some of the goods they had stolen from the town earlier in the day. They hadn't even reached Lexington, only 4 miles (6 km) from Concord, and it seemed as though they would have to surrender.

But as they approached the town they saw a full **brigade** of British troops, around one thousand men, under the command of Lord Percy. The reinforcements had finally arrived. Percy could not believe his eyes: there in front of him were the carefully selected British troops who had been specially trained. Luckily for the British, Percy had brought two cannons with him, and he had them set up on two hillsides overlooking Lexington. He burned some buildings, fearing that **snipers** were hiding in them.

Once Smith's troops had rested, Percy continued the retreat back to Boston. Along the way, his troops were attacked from behind every tree and wall, and from every window and door. As nightfall approached, Percy decided to turn toward Charlestown rather than Cambridge. If he headed for Cambridge, he would have been trapped: the patriots had dismantled the bridge into the town. Once the British limped into Charlestown, they took stock of their losses: 73 killed, 174 wounded, 28 missing. The patriots' casualties totaled 49 dead and 40 wounded or missing.

CHANGING THE COURSE OF HISTORY

April 19, 1775, was an amazing day. Colonists—farmers, merchants, artisans, and professionals—organized into an army, fired on 1,500 British troops, and kept them running for their lives, for 22 miles (35 km). Now there could be no turning back—the American Revolution had begun.

The patriots encircled the city of Boston. Word of the battles of Lexington and Concord spread to the other colonies, and colonists sent food, weapons, and men to the growing colonial army. Eventually, the ranks surrounding Boston swelled to ten thousand.

Less than a month after the battles of Lexington and Concord, the Second Continental Congress began meeting in Philadelphia. That same month, the patriots built a fort on a hill outside of Charlestown. The British attacked and barely defeated the patriots at the Battle of Bunker Hill. Meanwhile, the Second Continental Congress chose George Washington to recruit and train a colonial army. On July 4, 1776, thirteen colonies came together to form one country, and an experiment in democracy began that changed the course of history.

Glossary

boycotting—refusing to purchase or use certain goods or services

brigade—a unit of an army

clappers—the metal balls inside bells that strike against the sides when the bell is swung

dirge—a slow, solemn, and mournful piece of music

disbanded—dissolved, broken up

fasted—gave up eating for a period of time for an important, sometimes religious, purpose

flankers—soldiers positioned to protect the left or right sides of a column on a march

flint—a very hard, gray stone that makes sparks when steel is struck against it

incriminating—anything that would show someone is guilty of a crime or some wrongdoing

parsonage—minister's house

patriots—in the American Revolution, colonists who
rebelled against Britain

sexton—a person who takes care of church property

smuggling—taking something into or out of the country
illegally

snipers—people who shoot from a hidden place

tanner—a person who converts animal hides into leather

treason—the crime of betraying your country

vestryman—a member of a church who is elected to
manage the nonreligious duties of a congregation

Timeline: The Battles of

1773

MAY 10
Parliament passes the Tea Act.

DECEMBER 16
Patriots dressed as Mohawk Indians dump 342 chests of tea into Boston Harbor.

1774

As punishment for the Boston Tea Party, Parliament passes the Restraining Acts. The colonists nickname them the Intolerable Acts.

JUNE 1
The Boston Port Act goes into effect, closing down the port of Boston and most of the city's commerce with it.

OCTOBER
The First Continental Congress meets in Philadelphia and Massachusetts selects delegates to the Massachusetts Provincial Congress.

Lexington and Concord

1775

APRIL 18
The British are observed preparing to take some action. Paul Revere and Billy Dawes set out to warn the countryside of their approach.

APRIL 19
In action at Lexington Common, eight militiamen are killed. British troops retreating to Boston suffer more than 250 casualties.

MAY 10
The Second Continental Congress meets in Philadelphia and authorizes George Washington to recruit a colonial army.

JUNE 17
The first major battle of the American Revolution, the Battle of Bunker Hill, is fought. The British victory costs them 1,154 casualties to the colonists' 411.

To Find Out More

BOOKS

Bigelow, Barbara, and Linda Schmittroth. *American Revolution Almanac*. Detroit: UXL, 2000.

Fradin, Dennis Brindell. *Let It Begin Here! Lexington & Concord: First Battles of the American Revolution*. New York: Walker Books for Young Readers, 2005.

Hallahan, William H. *The Day the American Revolution Began*. New York: William Morrow, 2000.

Raatma, Lucia. *The Battles of Lexington and Concord*. Minneapolis: Compass Point Books, 2003.

Whitelaw, Nancy. *The Shot Heard Round the World: The Battles of Lexington and Concord*. Greensboro, N.C.: Morgan Reynolds, 2001.

ONLINE SITES

Battle of Concord
http://www.publicbookshelf.com/public_html/Our_Country_vol_2/ battlecon_fi.html

Golden Nuggets of U.S. History: The Old North Bridge, Concord, Massachusetts
http://www.franklaughter.web.aplus.net/bin/history/northbridge.html

Minuteman National Historical Park
http://www.nps.gov/mima/

Index

Bold numbers indicate illustrations.

About the Author

Heidi Kimmel is a children's book author and editor with a special interest in U.S. history. She lived in Boston for nine years, during which time she became fascinated by Massachusetts's role in the American Revolution and visited most of the sites mentioned in this book. She is also the author of another Cornerstones of Freedom book, *West Point*. She currently lives in Poughkeepsie, New York, with her husband, David, a dog, and two cats. Her two sons, Steven and Paul, are her inspiration.